The 1st Treasury of
HERMAN

Books in the Andrews and McMeel Treasury Series

The Family Circus Treasury by Bil Keane

The Ziggy Treasury by Tom Wilson

The Momma Treasury by Mell Lazarus

The Marmaduke Treasury by Brad Anderson

The Tank McNamara Chronicles by Jeff Millar and Bill Hinds

The Cathy Chronicles by Cathy Guisewite

Encore! Encore!! by Tom Wilson

The 1st Treasury of
HERMAN

by Jim Unger

Andrews and McMeel, Inc.
A Universal Press Syndicate Company
Kansas City • New York • Washington

ISBN: 0-8362-1121-9 cloth
0-8362-1122-7 paperback
Library of Congress Catalog Card Number 79-84409

First printing April 1979
Second printing July 1979
Third printing August 1979
Fourth printing October 1979
Fifth printing November 1979
Sixth printing December 1979
Seventh printing January 1980
Eighth printing April 1980

The key to happiness and freedom is a sense of humor and a sense of humor is nothing more or less than the ability to laugh at oneself.

—Jim Unger

1.

All you need to be a cartoonist is a sheet of paper, a two-dollar pen and a sense of humor. The sense of humor is especially important if, as in my case, it takes 30 years to save up the two dollars.

If dates are important, I started drawing Herman in 1974. I'd been doing some editorial cartoons for a Canadian newspaper more or less as a hobby but everybody kept laughing at them so much that they didn't read the editorials. So I got into comics. It was unnatural. I couldn't get used to the little square. Universal Press Syndicate took one look at what I'd drawn and said it was Herman. What do I know, I'd never even met the guy.

"D'you know 'Shine on Harvest Moon'?"

People are always asking me how I got started. I never tell them — especially if they can draw. If they draw really well and have a sense of humor, I always tell them I got started in the Army.

Actually, getting started isn't the hard part, it's dreaming up all the ideas day after day. Now that's hard. That's where it becomes necessary to resign from the human race and take a long hard look at things as they really are. You can't be objective about something to which you belong just as fish can't see the water in which they're swimming.

From earliest childhood our brains are programmed. We don't think, we learn. We learn what is happy and what is sad. We learn what is commonplace and we stop thinking about it anymore. We watch the clouds float across the sky and forget how strange they must have looked to us when we first saw them through the nursery window. I didn't have a nursery but I remember seeing them through a crack in the ceiling.

10

"Do you believe the nerve of that guy whistling at us like that?"

"He painted this one when he was 3 years old."

The essence of Herman humor is illustrating the comical behavior which all of us think of as normal. We all see the same things, do the same things and think the same thoughts. And when you think that everyone is trying to be an individual, that's funny to start with. Pope didn't have my gift of words but he once wrote:

"True wit is nature to advantage dress'd. What oft was thought, but ne'er so well express'd."

11

"Herman, your Doctor told you to
get away and RELAX."

"Do we need a set of encyclopedias?"

"Second serve."

"They've cured my Arthritis!"

"Herman, I can see perfectly well without a chair
to stand on . . . Herman!!!"

"That was HIS point."

"So much for camping!"

13

"He's not allowed out so I bought him a trampoline."

"Your boss says you can have the rest of the afternoon off . . ."

"You can't claim a world record unless it sticks in the grass."

"I don't want to ruin your day Herman but tomorrow morning I want to see you in my office."

"Okay, you can go now . . . they've evacuated the village."

"D'yer ever feel you're on the verge of an incredible breakthrough?"

"Herman, will you stop fooling around and finish cleaning these windows."

"Mind if we play through?"

15

"It says right here on the can, 'Do not use to clean overnight.'"

"Here's the coffee . . . right at the back."

"He's always the same when we go camping . . . wakes up and can't remember where he is."

"This model comes with shoulder straps for canoe trips; etc."

"How about a ten-minute 'shore-leave' to take out the garbage?"

"Herman, this is our deluxe comfort model."

"Let me put it this way . . . for your weight you should be thirty-seven feet tall."

"This toaster's gotta go back!"

17

"Starting tomorrow I don't want you to wash the 5,000 year old jugs!"

"Whadyer mean we don't need any brushes?"

"You'd better get a good grip on that net, Herman."

18

"I can imagine the fuss you'd make if I walked around dressed like that!"

"Herman . . . two is load . . . THREE is fire!"

"Now do you believe me Herman? . . . is that a sand-trap or is that a sand-trap?"

"Whadyer mean the needle's broken off?"

19

"Herman, don't go too far you'll miss Gunsmoke."

"Nice work Spike, you've hurt his arm."

"Two week's of jogging and so far he's made the front door."

"If she has one more birthday, this whole place is gonna go up!"

20

"This year I'm gonna finish off the basement!"

"Isn't it time he went to bed?"

"You spotted it, eh?"

"They think of everything...that's in case you forget your key."

"Why can't you dry your feet with a towel like everybody else?"

"Don't look at me...you gave him the carpentry set."

"Oh he hasn't escaped...he just gets these sudden cravings for a cheeseburger."

"Will that do?"

"Nice try!"

"Herman's so considerate when I'm sick...brought
the washer and dryer up to the bedroom."

"I think he wants to be friends!"

"Okay that's it...that's the last time he watches 'Kung Fu.'"

"No I don't know what sort it is but all my instincts tell me we should be about forty miles away when it hatches."

"Forgive the intrusion...I wonder if you'd mind telling the janitor the elevator's stuck?"

"Testing...testing...one, two, three."

"What was that?"

"She doesn't buy many luxuries but she loves her stereo."

"You'll have to practice somewhere else...
I want a shower."

"Will you quit shouting 'land on the starboard beam', while we're in port!"

"You go across the square, pass the nurse's residence, up the steps, through the main lobby...and second door on your left."

"It's getting so you can't trust anyone anymore."

"How many times have I told you to wear your helmet?"

"You're using my athlete's foot ointment."

"Okay...here's the results of your medical."

Now whatever happens, hang on to those sandwiches!"

"Okay Class...name four things he did wrong."

"Hey! Is there another word for 'Verily' that starts with a 'B'?"

"We'll take you off the vitamins for
a couple of days."

"Herman, I've never known a guy like you for
hitting them in the water."

"Abdul...will you keep that thing outa sight while
we're still in the oil business."

"I sometimes wonder if you hear one word I say!"

"Columbus, will yer sit down and stop asking all these dumb questions?"

"I can't explain now, but don't take your jacket off at work."

"I know it's your first day, but you've got to accept the fact that some customers are just 'lookers'."

"Can you send an ambulance to 27 Sycamore Drive in about six minutes?"

"Listen...if we get this right, we'll be famous."

"I'll never forget the time you strapped me for talking in class."

"Would it help any if I started sending your alimony weekly?"

"He's kicking my seat again...I thought you were going to say something?"

30

"Two million years ago, it ate nothing but caterpillars."

"Well, now we know what all that noise was about last night."

"This one's not signed."

"Members of the jury, have you reached a verdict?"

"I'll come back later when you're not busy."

"Have you got a window-seat?"

"Couldn't resist, could you?"

"Me and the boys were trying to guess how
you spell your name."

"That's it, perfect . . . keep it there."

"You ever known a day to drag like this?"

"Whadyer mean you wanna marry my daughter
. . . I thought you were my daughter!"

"I hope it's not inconvenient. We're your
new neighbors."

"Yeah, well as far as I'm concerned, bug killer is bug killer and you guys owe me a new screen door."

"Had any luck?"

"Are there any more 'income tax jokes' before we move on?"

"Listen, I gotta go. There's a guy waiting to use the phone."

"You the guy who ordered the 'Grand Slam' pizza?"

"Your mother warned me you'd start complaining about your food."

"Try to relax . . . he can smell fear."

"Had enough music?"

"I know you're in bed with the flu, but I need the keys to the filing cabinet."

"I thought you said you were coming home next Sunday"

"Keep in mind you're a guest on this bench."

"Ignore him. He knows he's due for his annual shots."

"Pity . . . would've made a nice set of luggage."

"Next door wants 'The Blue Danube.'"

"If you Jane, me Harry."

"I think I'm gonna need a couple of days off sick!"

"It doesn't matter what sort of dog you've got, Herman . . . it's guaranteed to keep away burglars."

"Six months at Art College and you say 'What's it s'posed to be?'"

"You can believe what you like . . . I tell you I saw one!"

"I'll give you two clues . . . we get Wild Kingdom on every channel and the cat's missing."

"Imagine those crooks wanting eleven bucks to fix this!"

"Can you remember where I bought this suit?"

"Your mother just phoned...she's coming over."

"Your boss says he's sorry but he can't come."

"I told him he needed more feathers."

"What did you spoil his tiger trap for...?"

'How d'yer want your eggs... black or dark brown?"

40

"He's doing two weeks 'solitary'!"

"What are the chances of becoming a pirate?"

"Here...make a wish."

"Has he had his dinner?"

"Can't you cook yourself something when I'm out?"

"It says; 'Come in number 10, your hour's up!'"

"Er, Doc...can he have a quick look at your diploma?"

"You wouldn't believe how tough it is to get him up in the morning."

"Don't sit on the bean-bag chair...it's got a split in it."

"Why don't you wear long socks 'til he learns to tell the difference?"

"Allow me to introduce myself...I'm a basketball talent scout."

"Stop complaining. How often does she get to see a drive-in movie?"

"HERMAN...did you forget to water my plants while I was away?"

"According to this quiz, you're a 'male chauvinist pig'."

"I really look forward to your cheery little visits."

"That's fine!"

"Just you start something. My husband's a karate expert."

"Sorry!"

"I'm glad their Apollo program is over, I was getting sick of taking this net down every five minutes."

"Seeing you once a month is gonna make
the next two years a lot easier."

"Cold lunch today . . . I'm going out."

"Nothing to declare."

"Next."

"Did you know your front wheel fell off?"

"Boy! . . . you sure know how to break a vow of silence."

"One seat at the front and one at the back."

"It's supposed to be macaroni pudding."

"George makes all our own furniture."

"In two days I'll owe $3,000.00 on a library book I haven't even read."

"I thought while I was getting the fuses, I'd pick up a few groceries."

"Five bucks if you start practicing your violin."

"I plugged it in to see if you'd fixed it."

"Did you get your raise?"

"I can always tell when they're wearing 'elevator shoes.'"

"Just as I thought...you need a new picture tube!"

"I don't care how much he likes Jacques Cousteau, I wanna watch baseball."

"Is there anything you need before I go?"

"It's the cook's coffee-break, so eat your dessert first."

50

"Nine and three-quarters...nine and seven-eighths..."

"We'll take a brief pause for this important commercial message."

"Oh no, he's weightlifting again."

"I know I'm scraping the barrel, but d'yer wanna dance?"

"As your Latin professor, I can't say you've exactly made my day."

"Forget it. I'm never gonna get THAT hungry."

"I said 'I wanna marry your daughter when I get some money' and he gave me twenty bucks."

"Happy birthday...I dropped your cake."

"Hope you sent Johnny Carson the bill for the lumber."

"Of course you don't lose YOUR ball...you never hit it more than six feet."

"If you let it go maybe it'll stop screaming."

"Sorry to keep you both waiting out here. Where's your wife?"

"If I've gotta do typing and stuff like that, I want more money!"

"We are now joining our regularly scheduled commercials which are already in progress."

"I know it's your first time in 38 years, but what would happen if everyone was ten minutes late for work?"

"Have a good vacation. I've decided not to give you your bad news until you get back."

"This t.v. dinner's got wires in it!"

"WAIST EIGHTY-TWO."

"Hey, come and see this. There's a guy been on strike for two years and he can't remember where he works."

"Two of these just fell out of the car."

"If you took my advice you'd throw away those bathroom scales. You're letting this weight-loss thing become an obsession."

"SLOW DOWN...WATCH THAT PUSSY CAT... TURN RIGHT HERE."

"What happened! Did I touch a nerve?"

"Is that the tie I bought him for Christmas?"

"Night work! You mean when it's dark?"

"Sure it's big, but it'll do an average room in three minutes."

"Is that the only way you can have a good time, smashing up public property?"

"The art teacher told us not to get disheartened if our first portrait looked like a hippopotamus with a hat on."

"That's a relief. I thought I'd gone deaf!"

"I found him working in the stockroom, J. D. He's perfect!"

"HIPPY!"

"Writing your autobiography! Who's it about?"

"Any other complaints?"

"You've DEFINITELY got the flu."

"I'm the baby-sitter. Where's the fridge?"

"Plain black! Hey that's groovy man—plain black boots!"

"FIRED! Does that mean I won't get the raise?"

"I'm getting sick of this arm wrestling to see who does the rotten dishes."

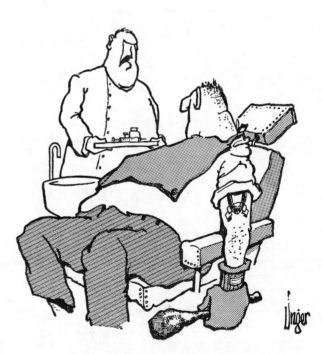

"Don't worry, this'll probably hurt me more than you."

"She gets nervous when we use the new cups."

"I know it's sudden—but I want a divorce!"

"I think we're in trouble. He doesn't even know what a car is!"

"Your mother's out in the yard."

I was born in London, England. We weren't allowed newspapers in the ward so I wasn't sure of the exact date. I know I'm "Aquarius."

I wanted to be a judge when I was eleven. Then I wanted to be an architect, then a pilot, then a judge again. I never ever wanted to be a cartoonist. I wasn't funny and I couldn't draw. Ideal qualifications for a judge.

I had a pretty average childhood. The Second World War broke out when I was two. I tried to join up but they made me sit it out in an air-raid shelter. Every kid on the street could tell the dif-

"The jury has found you not guilty, but I'm going to give you 2 years just to be on the safe side."

ference between a Lancaster and a Heinkel at 20,000 feet. After the war things started to get tough. I had to go to a boy's grammar school. No girls, just five hundred boys, all dressed the same in maroon blazers, gray flannel slacks and a maroon cap with gold rings around it. It was tough being an individual in those days. I used to wear a false moustache.

I think I got my first real insight into the human condition when I was dragged off kicking and screaming into the British Army for two years. Every soldier I ever knew spent 95 percent of his energies writing love letters to his girlfriend and 5 percent running up and down obstacle courses and mopping floors. So much for war!

W.S. Gilbert, another one who had trouble putting things down on paper, once wrote: "Man is Nature's sole mistake." I think what he meant was that *his perception* of man was Nature's sole mistake.

"I can't remember the last time you put your arm around me at the movies."

If you saw a hippopotamus and everyone around you convinced you it was a racehorse, you'd think it was a pretty ugly racehorse. Taken one step further, if they convinced you it was a French poodle, it would be even uglier. In fact, it was probably a pretty nifty hippo. So that's what I do in Herman. I draw the hippos. They're really quite lovable.

"Don't spill this; it's goldfish."

"MISSED!"

"Where's a U.F.O.?"

"It'll take you a couple of days to get used to these express elevators."

"Watch out...the plate's hot."

"Is that your idea of 20 pounds of potatoes?"

"Try to guess who this is for..."

"ONE."

"Going up the Amazon?"

"I think I'll sell all my jewelry. I need the five dollars."

"My, my...you're the image of your father!"

"34-24-36...It sounds like your right arm."

"How come I have to pay the same air fare as a great lump like him?"

"What'sa matter with you...doncha like spaghetti?"

"Sure, I'd love a second honeymoon...who with?"

"Will you quit arguing and give me my seven iron."

"Watch out for his screw-ball."

69

"It'll take you a couple of days to get used to them."

"Sounds like a power struggle between the spaghetti and the pickled onions."

"Want me to wrap it?"

"Want mashed potatoes?"

"I admire initiative, but when I want a 'funnel' I mean one of these."

"How much longer did he tell you to stay on this banana diet?"

"Get up, you idiot. When I say, 'how do you plead?' I wanna know if you're 'guilty' or 'not guilty'."

"That new guy was supposed to be helping me roll this."

"Haven't you got a brush?"

"Hold it! They're out of season."

"Your four aces don't beat my two eights unless you've got a red king!"

"Think it'll work?"

"Try to relax."

"You're supposed to say 'I do' not 'I'll try.'"

"Did you sleep okay, Herman?"

73

"Did you win?"

"All I said was I didn't want it in stereo."

"Did he make you buy anything?"

"'One Hundred and One Ways to Rip Off Credit Companies'... is that cash or charge?"

"I've changed my mind. I'll have a
cheese sandwich."

"What song did you sing?"

"Don't forget to lock up when you
leave, Henderson."

"I'd expect it from the younger generation, but
asking for more money at your age is
absolutely inexcusable."

75

"Can I take them with water?"

"I'll work my way up your arm and you tell me when you feel anything."

"Show me that piece of paper again with the calculations on it."

"You're not Robert Redford."

"So that's your story—you hate to be late!"

"The man we're looking for will be dynamic and aggressive."

"You'd never get to the moon. You'd need two hundred of those things."

"There, you leave your toys all over the floor and now Mommy can't watch her favorite program."

"Three nights in a row I've dreamt you were Dracula."

"Do I get that one again?"

"He loves a cup of tea."

"I read somewhere that expensive champagne doesn't go 'pop.'"

"I don't care if it is plastic. I could have had a heart attack."

"Have you got any others with more spikes?"

"The sporting goods store phoned. You left your hat on the counter."

"Where did they get him from?"

"Madam, giving your husband 'twenty years in the slammer' is not my idea of a divorce settlement.'

"Why don't you start climbing out and I'll keep trying the buttons."

"Whaddya making?"

"STAMPEDE!"

"Shall I turn it off?"

"I'm your anesthetist and he's my 'back-up man'."

"Your wife took the new baby home in a cab
an hour ago."

"You're certainly enjoying my little cakes. Have
another one!"

"Bermuda triangle."

"You MUST know how you got in there."

"Slice of wedding cake?"

"I take it you don't want any of this cheese."

"I'll only be gone for a month, so don't use the kitchen."

"There goes my tip, right?"

"Members of the jury, I ask you—does my client look like a man of violence?"

"Here, you wanted a shark's-tooth necklace.
Dig those outa my leg."

"Saturday evenings with you are a real treat."

"If I don't get a pay-raise soon, I'm gonna
blow the lid off this crummy zoo."

"That's just his way of saying he wants you to stay!"

"Size what?"

"Tomorrow morning I'm having you adopted."

"Oh, it's you! I thought it was a burglar."

"D'you get the feeling one of us is getting ripped-off?"

85

"I'll count to three, then I'm gonna use the sink."

"That pain-in-the-neck's out here, doctor."

"Don't forget to mark it 'Personal.'"

"Aren't you going to phone the airport?"

"When we say 'parents invited' we usually mean to sit and watch."

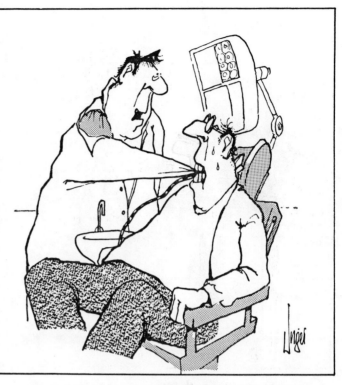

"I promise no more drilling if you let go."

"Chicken for breakfast, chicken for lunch, chicken for dinner. What d'you expect?"

"Okay, you've got five minutes to capture my interest."

"I'll be home soon; I'm at the Speedy Shoe Repair Boutique."

"Whaddyer mean, 'Which one is ours?'"

"Pretend you're a purse snatcher, I wanna try something."

"Listen, I've got to go. Give my love to everyone in Australia."

88

"Why don't you start going to bed earlier?"

"Are you eating properly and getting plenty of exercise?"

"Is that everything, just a bar of soap?"

"For crying out loud! If it's that important to you, take the afternoon off."

"Want me to get you a shopping cart?"

"I called earlier but your wife said you hadn't got the brains to read these books."

"Okay, take a break!"

"As I was saying, this company offers excellent retirement benefits."

"Hey, GET OFF MY LAND!"

"The cat had a fit!"

"First things first. Get your stomach off my desk."

"Are you going to drink this coffee or shall I throw it away?"

"Here, don't touch the stick."

"If you're going to wear that coat, I think you could use a lighter shade."

"Why don't you buy a proper set of headphones?"

"Commander, how does it feel to be back on earth after six months of weightlessness?"

"This idiot opened all the windows halfway
through the car wash."

"He's got a wicked slice!"

"Look in my sister's blue bag."

"I don't think I'll bother with a tan 'til I get out."

"You always said you liked it strong."

"Get out! I haven't forgotten I fired you this morning."

"STAY!"

94

"Why don't you go to a proper dentist?"

"If you read the instructions, dummy, you'd see there's one switch for drying and another for styling."

"If you've got any screaming to do, wait until you get off the premises."

"Now, imagine you've cornered a bear and he runs into a disused house."

"I think it's the T. V. repairman."

"Don't you want your receipt?"

"If this marriage is going to work, you're going to have to learn to control your temper."

"All I said was, 'Open your suitcase.'"

96

"You're looking a lot better today, Ralph."

"And you wonder why I never want to go to Italian restaurants!"

"The results of your tests were negative. Get lost!"

"That was a good idea, sending out for a pizza while the elevator's on the fritz."

"All bets are off if you don't quit laughing."

"It was supposed to be Mom, but I messed it up."

"Your wife phoned. She said if you want toast for breakfast, bring home a loaf of bread!"

"Try to imagine how much I care!"

"It just says, 'Windows repaired—five bucks.'"

"His English teacher says he's a groovy, far-out kid."

"You're fighting the King in the semi-finals, so just duck once and he won't get too tired."

"You must have run a mile this time—you've been gone four minutes."

"This is your last chance. If you scalp this one,
you're through."

"I've got two other applicants to see before I
make my final choice."

"Even as a kid I was a slow eater."

"Don't laugh, my wife thinks I'm in South
America with two million bucks."

"How would you like to eat off the floor every day?"

"We're not gonna charge you for this first lesson."

"Got any books on dog training?"

"Did you shake the bottle?"

101

"You're looking at it upside down!"

"Don't go rushing into marriage. Look around for a couple of years like your mother did."

"Who's calling? D'you know what time it is?"

"Does that hurt?"

"He's getting better. He can remember everything now except getting married."

"What did he mean, 'Love is blind'?"

"If you remember, I did mention possible side-effects."

"How come I get a different driving
instructor every week?"

"I told you he wouldn't eat that ice cream."

"Did you feel the earthquake?"

"You've got Egyptian flu. You're going to be a
'mummy.'"

"Normally I ignore things said to me in fun at the Christmas party, however ..."

"Don't blame me. I was cleaning his cage and he flew up the pipe."

"You're washing the floor with tomorrow's soup-of-the-day!"

"Memorize this, it's your New Year resolutions."

"I cut a piece off the bottom and patched your shirt."

"Herm, want me to make a little hole and feed you some grapes?"

"Fifteen years is not so long. You've already done 12 days."

"Well, well, my secret file tells me that since 1948 this is your grandmother's seventh funeral."

"I got fantastic references from my last five jobs but I lost them on the way over here."

"Hope it's not too dry."

"We're gonna have supper as soon as you shove off."

"Smarten up! Sometimes I think your father's got more brains than you have."

"Let's face it; if you'd really loved me, you'd have married someone else!"

"He's a self-made man."

"You've got an hour to paint your nails and an hour to talk to your mother. I'm going to a meeting."

"According to this, you've been having a back problem."

"Of course I care for you. Money and looks aren't everything you know!"

"Do you have to keep saying 'bunch of junk' every five minutes. I'm enjoying it!"

"Wake up, Daddy."

"QUIT SHOVING!"

"Come along, Polly. Let Mr. Herman finish his coffee."

"All the clocks have stopped!"

"See that! I forgot to tighten the nut."

"Whaddyer mean 'checkmate'? Get to bed."

"Why don't you let your husband go to the ball game?"

"He thinks we're muggers!"

"Take it easy, take it easy. I've come to fix the window."

"A truck ran over my cast!"

"This is my first day. Do we get paid?"

"You're my last hope, Harry. Can I borrow your dinner jacket?"

"Will ya take a check?"

"For the tenth time, I'm NOT going bowling."

"Debbie looks exactly like me when I was 18."

"D'yer like that blue?"

"I thought I'd put in a little vegetable garden."

"I'll leave you to park the car, I'm going to bed."

"How long have you had your feet on the wrong legs?"

"Maybe you're beginning to get the message that we need a recreation room."

"Don't look at me like that, I was polishing it."

"If I can't get a summer job this year I think I'll get married."

"There...now argue!"

"This is Blue Buzzard, good buddy; Smokey's
on the warpath."

"If I have to keep going to school, all the best
jobs are gonna be snapped up."

"I thought you told me we didn't give
'cash refunds.'"

3.

Who is Herman anyway? Which one is he? Well he's all of them and yet you never see him. He's in make-up. Just as an actor becomes a part for a movie so Herman's physical characteristics become an integral part of the comic. The humor is supremely important, the characters are secondary to the situation. Aside from all that, I can't draw the same person twice anyway. I told you I couldn't draw!

"We can put all our old junk up here."

Sometimes I agonize for hours trying to think up those daily "situations." Some days are a complete blank and some days I'll think of ten in an hour. I just lounge around in front of the television and scribble. If there's a good program showing, I scribble slower. As soon as I have 36 scribbles ready I crawl out of the armchair or off the sofa and slowly make my way to the drawing board. It's only about fifteen feet away but it sometimes takes four weeks to get there. I spend a week drawing and inking and living like a monk. Thirty-six seems like an awful lot of comics especially when working on the first one. I'm usually about ten heartbeats away from a nervous breakdown when I finally finish the six-weeks batch and I can't wait to get them in the envelope and mail them off. As soon as they're away I usually fall

"He's still there! I wish you wouldn't over-tip like
that."

"I hope I'm facing in this direction when I wake up
in the morning."

down outside the Post Office and lay there panting
for a couple of hours. If it's cold I pant inside. I
wouldn't want you to think it's easy.

For the technically minded, I use white paper
and black ink.

119

"I see you're taking a trip."

"If you keep bugging me about getting married, I'm gonna break off our engagement."

"You've got to start sometime. Why don't you operate on this one?"

"I knew you hadn't quit!"

"We're both a lot better since the doctor gave
me something for my nerves."

"Okay, Racquel, but what are you gonna
tell my wife?"

"Whose turn was it to put the stupid dog out
last night?"

"If you want your money back, say so! Don't give
me that guff about it being too noisy."

"Hang on to your tickets! You may have trouble bringing that kid out."

"Leave the car keys just in case something grabs you out there."

"Another good feature of this home is that it's within a stone's throw of several schools."

"Stop whining. I caught it so I'll carry it."

"GET YOUR ELBOWS OFF THE TABLE!"

"No one said the job was gonna be a bed of roses."

"You'd better stay off solid food for an hour or two."

"Ouch!"

"That must have been one heavy suitcase!"

"I hate to mention it but there was a $1.80 on the meter when I hit that truck."

"Your son-in-law's not here this afternoon. He's gone to your funeral."

"How are you getting on with the diet?"

"I wanted to leave you a tip but I haven't got change for a quarter."

"You dropped it. You get it!"

"Where do you think you get off taking out your own appendix?"

"Will you shove off. I'm sick of your jealousy!"

125

"GET LOST."

"I think he's trying to tell us he can't paint!"

"How could I have been doing 70 miles an hour when I've only been driving for ten minutes?"

"You can start tomorrow, but as soon as my wife sees you you're finished!"

"Keep going! I'll run out and mortgage the house and meet you at the check-out."

"If you were a horse we could have shot yer!"

"Don't keep saying you don't like them. You've only had them on for five minutes."

"I don't mind a long wait in here; the food's terrible."

"Come in, Coach. I wanna discuss your
lifetime contract."

"I'm just gonna say my prayers. D'yer
need anything?"

"You mean I've gotta pay tax on money I've
already spent?"

"I wanna open a joint-account with someone
who's got plenty of dough."

"The bank wants to lend us five thousand bucks to get out of debt!"

"...and don't call me illiterate. My Ma and Pa have been married for thirty-eight years."

"He wants a blue dress for his wife, size 'fat.'"

"Where's the kids?"

"FORE."

"I appreciate that this is only your first day at the zoo, but from now on just paint the empty cages."

"As I see it, you've got a choice between a 'birdie' and promotion to branch manager."

"Set the clock for 5:30!"

"He wouldn't eat it so I put in some dirt and made it look like mud."

"The way you carry on, you'd think I enjoy these business trips."

"Mom said we can get married and live in the dining room if you don't mind eating in the kitchen."

"Can't you ever get sick without bringing home one of those?"

"LADIES AND GENTLEMEN, the bride and groom!"

"They don't give us time to learn anything; we have to listen to the teacher all day."

"I see you've listed your hobbies as alpine skiing, scuba, sky-diving, treasure hunting and climbing Mount Everest."

"GET OFF THAT OILY MAN WITH YOUR BEST SHOES ON."

"I can do shorthand! It just takes a little longer."

"Look what your stupid uncle gave us. What d'yer think it is?"

"If you're so dead-set against gambling, how come you're still in the marriage business?"

"Judy, are you gonna elope or not?"

133

"Sure you can have it for ten bucks, but wouldn't you rather own a $200 painting?"

"Congratulations! He seems very bright."

"Mr. Harrison took-off for South America with the company pay-roll. D'yer wanna leave a message?"

"Everyone in the building got together. Here's 200 bucks for your violin."

"Sure it's faded! You've been wearing it during daylight hours without a jacket on."

"Well, if you didn't rob the bank, how are you gonna pay my fee to prove your innocence?"

"Well, now we know who's been swiping your hormone pills."

"You're sure I'll be able to swim with it?"

"We can't live with my parents. They're still living with their parents!"

"I decided to come in today. The poolroom's packed."

"Is this your first blind date?"

"And another thing! I'm getting sick of you being so agreeable all the time."

"I'd ask for a doggie-bag but my doggie wouldn't eat that if I paid him."

"Are you sure you're comfortable?"

"You've got six wives waiting for you on the outside. Are you sure you want a parole?"

"I don't wanna be a juror! Can't I be a witness?"

"For Pete's sake, don't sit behind her when we get inside."

"Is it still raining?"

"Just take a seat, son. You're next."

"Don't worry about my punctuation. I'll be here at exactly nine o'clock every morning."

"Mr. Henderson, he's written another check!"

"Listen, there's nothing wrong with being ambitious."

"Browning, for a guy who's worked here 12 years, you're setting a lousy example."

"They say opposites attract. There must be plenty of good-looking, intelligent girls around."

"'F' means 'fantastic.'"

"The sink's backed up!"

"I'm NOT going camping. If you wanna get back to nature, take the bug screen out of the window for half an hour."

"Okay, you've got your 'nose job.' Now get out there and meet girls."

"You can't be expected to get it right first time!"

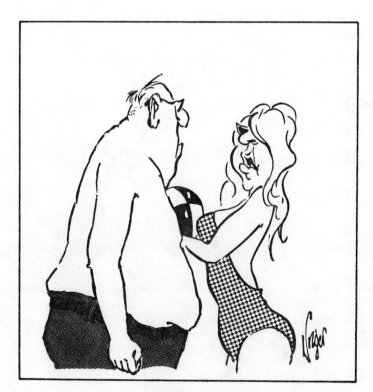

"Boy, Harry, you sure look different without your wallet!"

"Next time you go to the store, get some proper paper napkins."

"It's called 'Pigeons Beware.'"

"I told you to use my insect spray."

"Did she tell you I got a job down at
the fish market?"

"Look what she did to my candy bar!"

142

"The Marquis of Halifax writes, 'The vanity of teaching doth oft tempt man to forget he is a blockhead'."

"I hope you used warm water. I don't want to listen to those things chattering all night."

"He's got your hair!"

"Hey, Harry! Look at this guy's wife."

"Did you say this pizza gave you indigestion?"

"How sweet! A nice little card for my twenty-first birthday!"

"Do you think the current economic policies will do anything to ease the overall unemployment picture and dampen inflation?"

"It's a piece of wood!"

"Four months, eight days, five hours and twenty minutes. Four months, eight days, five hours and nineteen minutes."

"Don't do that while I'm eating!"

"Hospital regulations. You gotta wear the straps while I read the bill."

"How does it feel to take some little kid's last fifteen cents in the whole world?"

"Butcher Harris is doing this one tomorrow morning."

"My sister just gave me two dollars not to tell you something."

"I haven't got those in a twelve but I can let you have a couple of pair of size sixes."

"I'm sorry. I thought you were my husband."

"My wife wants to read for a while so I thought I'd watch you guys."

"So I said to her, 'how about giving me something to remember you by?'"

"I wish you hadn't worn that tie. It doesn't go with your jacket."

"As most of you know, our company treasurer won't be with us for the next fifteen annual meetings."

"Ma! I just met this new guy. He's not good-looking or anything but he's an accountant."

"It's okay! I found the keys."

"I'm sure you'll agree, we don't want an epidemic."

"How come every time we have company, I get stuck with this chair?"

"I haven't understood one word you said. Come back when your face gets better."

"If you only want to spend five dollars, I'd recommend two hamburgers and a three buck tip."

"That bit about 'Love, honor and obey.' Is that me or her?"

"Hey Pop! Your hearing aid has slipped down the leg of your pants!"

"Why don't you listen. I said you need a chiropractor not choir practice!"

"What exactly is 'new, improved lettuce?'"

"Hey Tex. Come and settle an argument. Is this arrow Apache or Sioux?"

"If you're gonna stay like that all weekend, I think you'd better start smoking again."

"Grannie, your horoscope says be prepared for a whirlwind romance!"

"D'you realize we've been married three whole weeks and neither of us has even mentioned the word 'divorce.'"

"You're not supposed to just pour the stew into the lunch pail."

"You got nothing to smile about."

"Breakfast in bed, your majesty."

"Don't move while I'm gone. You'll spill my drink."

THINK THIN

"I've had a hard day, so don't make any smart remarks while I'm carrying a cream pie."

"I see you've fixed the drip!"

"I thought T.V. was supposed to make you violent!"

"Can't you get on with your work without watching me all the time?"

"You said you didn't mind tea or coffee so I gave you half and half!"

"He left everything to the one woman who sustained him through his later years; Farah Fawcett Majors."

"He says you gotta go to bed and take a couple of aspirins."

"I'm not the world's greatest cook but I think you'll enjoy my cornflakes."

"You wasted all day taking this film and it's blank!"

"I told him he could have your 'left-overs.'"

"I wish you'd let me know you were coming in here. I had to throw away a perfectly good frozen dinner."

"If you get up a little earlier, you'd have more time to shave!"

"WHERE are you? I thought you were gonna put a new lock on this door?"

"Oh goody! You found my comb."

"I know your landlord depends on the rent but you still can't list him as a dependent."

"If I'm innocent 'til proven guilty,' why can't I buzz off to Australia and you let me know how things turn out?"

"I told her I wanted a 'trial separation' so she tried to separate my shoulder!"

"You're not allowed to be a grandfather anymore; you're a 'grandperson.'"

"Okay, just once more then it's bedtime."

"Hey Mom. I got that job. Get over here quick and show me what to do."

"I spilt the stupid plant food."

"I know the same thing happened last year. I'm 'accident prone.'"

"I had to dig it all by hand."

"I'm well aware it's only a plastic sword. Don't interfere!"

"Hey lady! If you keep your rollers lined up with the screen, I'll be able to watch the movie."

"It's baked turkey. The feathers got a bit black."

"I'm not sneering at your qualifications. I just wasn't aware you could get a B.A. for 'flower arrangement!'"

"I'm just showing these guys around the place."

"I asked that Doctor over there what he would take to cure a stomach upset and he said about $85.00."

"I still have to give you a ticket."

"We been to the museums."

"You sure that's beef?"

"You can go to the convention if you're lucky enough to make it through this door."

"Pssst...D'you wanna buy a burglar-proof lock?"

"And in recognition of your 20 years loyal service in the X-ray department..."

"He gets me out for a little exercise!"

"If that's supposed to improve your looks, it worked!"

"Have you finished with that?"

"If they ever edit this for television, it'll run about two minutes."

"You after another pay raise?"

"Both your eardrums are showing definite signs of rejection. How long have you worked in a disco?"

"Why didn't you say you wanted a sandwich while I was in the kitchen?"

"Are you coming hunting, or are you gonna sit around here all day inventing?"

"What sort of dog eats carrots?"

"We're short of plates!"

163

"Grandma, I can see where Dad gets his whiskers!"

"This one's supposed to go, 'snap, crackle, BOOM!'"

"You didn't forget to pay the window-cleaner again?"

"I've got the results of your X-rays."

"The TV won't be ready 'til next Friday."

"Look, as soon as a private room becomes available, you'll get one."

"Is it OK if I scratch my ear?"

"That one's automatic!"

"Everything's cut-and-dried with you isn't it? Even baby-sitting!"

"I don't know how you manage to eat all my cooking and never put on any weight."

"You wait! As soon as someone discovers gravity, they'll all come down and hit the ground."

"You asked us to build a computer which could replace the government."

"You in one of your moods again?"

"It looks better in the other room."

"It's a big step—getting married. You'll have to
give me some time to think about it. What was
your name again?"

"Look at my rug! I told you not to put exploding
cheese down the mouseholes."

"I was cleaning it!"

"How much longer you gonna be in this bathroom?"

"It took me three hours, but I finally discovered why you're limping. You lost the heel off your shoe."

"I think he takes after his great great great great great great great great great-grandfather."

"I can't find my clean underwear."

"It'll go away if you don't keep looking at it."

"Whaddyer mean, it's only a model? How much bigger d'you wanna build it?"

"Good morning, sir. Is your wife home?"

I live in Ottawa. It's a beautiful city and both my parents and my brothers and sisters all live in close proximity. I suppose I could live almost anywhere in the world but I'm happy being around the family and you can't draw comics if you're not happy. It gets cold and white in the winter but the snow can be fun. I bought a pair of skis last year. I haven't used them much but I look at them a lot. I also look at my ice skates when I'm not looking at the skis and in the summer I look at the tennis racket I bought two years ago.

My main hobbies are watching television and taking hot baths.

Sometimes I paint a picture when there's nothing good on or when I'm too clean.

"If you don't buy one of these pencils, you're placing an unfair burden on the rest of society."

Mostly I like traveling. Driving traveling and flying traveling. I love highways and airports, gas stations and jets. When I'm not anguishing over Herman I like to be on the move anywhere. When I get to wherever I'm going I want to come back.

You know, it's a great way to make a living, drawing comics and making people laugh. Like other creative professions, it requires a lot of self-discipline to work hard at something all alone. It takes getting used to, not driving ten miles to work at eight o'clock every morning with a bag of sandwiches. I don't have to be on time each day. I don't have someone watching over me, I can't get fired and I don't have to contribute to a pension plan. I really miss all that!

"No wonder your brother never writes!"

"The rear-view mirrors are my idea;
just until your neck gets better."

When people ask me about the future I think of more Hermans. It's quite a challenge to come up with better comics all the time. The drawing is getting slicker and I never worry about running out of ideas. After all, I've got four billion Hermans working for me every day.

I don't know what I want to do when I grow up.

"Hold still! I dropped my little mirror."

"They wouldn't let people stand here if it was dangerous."

"Hermy, either we're gonna get married or I guess I shouldn't see you any more."

"Fifteen years up already?"

"You're not gonna putt 387 yards?"

"If we don't go to the zoo tomorrow, you'd better get yourself a good lawyer."

"I told you on the phone she had a lot of hair."

"Da-da! One wig. Everybody owes me five cents."

175

"I wouldn't know a 'home-run' if I saw one."

"You say you were helping your husband
move furniture and it just 'locked'?"

"It's a guy from the zoo calling from across
the street."

"I can't see any sense in this! We passed about 10
fish markets on the way here."

176

"D'you wanna give any money to save Norwegian crocodiles?"

"How's it going? I'd heard you quit your job at the bank."

"Keep those press and t.v. people out of here 'til we've had a chance to explain what's wrong with him."

"I'm so desperate for a job, I'll even start at the bottom if it's absolutely necessary."

"Did I hear you right? Did you just tell me I'm starting to put on weight?"

"I haven't changed much since I was 18, have I?"

"While you're taking time off from work, just remember where you got the germs."

"I bet your mother's pie wasn't as soft as that."

"That too tight?"

"You're not making any sense! First you say your wife ran off with your best friend and then you tell us you never actually met the guy."

"You mustn't stand here looking so bored. You're supposed to be having a good time!"

"Can you send someone over? The t.v.'s making a high-pitched whistling sound."

"So sorry I woke you!"

"He's trying to figure out a way to clone himself so he can stay home all day and still get a paycheck."

"You say it was silver, cigar-shaped and had the letters U.F.O. painted on the side?"

"How is it I take a shower every day and do it without stepping on the soap?"

"It's been brought to my attention that you retired from here in 1948. I just want to know where you get the nerve to draw a company pension for 30 years."

"We were discussing separate vacations last night. Sorry about all the noise!"

"Look at the dopey names on this menu! What's an 'elk-burger'?"

"What's a good hand signal for backing onto a freeway?"

"Thanks for looking after the bird while I was away."

"Nice tackle, Ron! I think you'll make the team."

"I'm still awake, you know!"

"Grab his legs!"

"There's a guy at the door wants to know what I think of 'women's lib.' What shall I tell him?"

"I phoned your office and they didn't even know you were off sick."

"Your wife is still under the anesthetic and from what I've heard, this would be a good time to see her."

"It says 'parental guidance recommended.' You gonna call your mother?"

"Meadows, the doctor says I need more exercise, so I want you to start jogging for me."

"Get this straight! If people only retire when they're no longer productive, you should've gone 10 years ago!"

"If my dad asks you what you do for a living, say you're a marine biologist!"

"If you don't go to sleep, you're gonna be practicing that swing in a wheelchair."

"Dearly beloved, as this is John's third wedding and Betty's second, I'll make this as brief as possible."

"Gesundheit!"

"How am I supposed to watch television when he's always wearing my glasses?"

"This room you gave me overlooking the ocean. Is that the Pacific, the Atlantic or the Arctic?"

"Will I what?"

"I've seen a lot of those big lumpy things since we got here—but so far, no real people."

"I was gonna give you fresh garden peas but I couldn't find the can opener."

"I finally tracked down your records. I had them in the 'dead' file."

"His teacher wants you to bake a cake for him to take to school. Must be a geology lesson."

"It's the results of that cooking competition. You've been awarded a 'black belt.'"

"Take a look up the road and see if my boss is coming. A little ugly guy with a bald head."

"What was that clown next door saying about building a new closet?"

"Harry can't reach the drum!"

"Supper ready?"

"When you told me on the phone you were 42, 22, 38 I didn't realize you meant your age, your I. Q., and your shoe size."

"The forecast said there's a 50 percent chance of rain so genius is watering half the lawn."

188

"Move over a bit. I can't see the Grand Canyon."

"Don't forget it's my mother's birthday tomorrow."

"I'm well aware you're only 28 years old. That's why I'm telling you to take better care of yourself."

"Teacher says if I don't do well at school, I'll end up like you."

"Did you see where that one went?"

"Look at my wall! Can't you tell the difference between bug-killer and spray-paint?"

"I didn't like the look of that fish when I gave it to him."

"I wish you wouldn't keep reading while I'm trying to watch T V"

"I guess you don't read so good."

"Close the account? You mean you want to draw out the whole 90 cents?"

"A car or boat, maybe; but I'm not lending you money for food."

"What are you up to?"

"You the young fella thinking of buying the farm?"

"Just the usual full-moon crowd."

"I know it's expensive to bring up a kid. Why come to me with your problems?"

"Linda, those men's pants we had on sale—were they machine-washable?"

192

"Harry across the street says we've got a big silver thing parked on our roof."

"How many guys d'you know with a solar-powered wristwatch?"

"Can you turn this way a little bit?"

"Whiplash!"

"I'm putting you on probation. That means no
more mugging for 12 months."

"His bark's a lot worse than his bite."

"When I was your age, I was the only one to have
an engagement ring that squirted water."

"Every summer we get another rash of
'Littlefoot' sightings."

"Piano movers!"

"Can we use this as a picnic table?"

"Mom found your credit cards under the mattress
and she's gone shopping."

"I hope you never need a brain transplant. It'll be
rejected."

195

"Hidden camera commercial, take 9."

"Have what you like up to $1.50."

"Dentistry's come a long way in the last few years."

"I'll take a check if you've got some identification."

196

"You come 50 million miles and all you can tell me is, 'Stick that meat on the fire; it'll taste better'?"

"When they invented the first clock, how did they know what time to set it?"

"Visiting hours are 2 'til 4 p.m."

"You can't blame tv if you're dumb enough to walk up to a 300-lb. truck driver and say, 'Ring around the collar.'"

"The capital of Holland is 'H.'"

"If you'd buy me a dishwasher, you'd have more time to help out around here."

"Well, at least we now know why you were a cook in the navy!"

"I know it's only our first date, but I've got this crazy feeling that we were made for each other."

"I'll have to open you up again: That watch has great sentimental value."

"Your stupid manager from work came over to see how you were so I told him to get lost."

"You wouldn't believe the dream I just had."

"You only want me to get a haircut because you're jealous."

"Even if they have got it in your size, it'll cost at least a hundred bucks."

"How DARE you shout at me like that in front of the plants."

"Which floor?"

"Every time we go out anywhere, you always find something to complain about."

200

"False alarm. Your wife had an inflamed gall-bladder."

"Well, the window's open. I hope you're satisfied."

"Would you believe it? I've been all over town trying to get you some flowers."

"I guess I can borrow a magnifying glass to show it to the girls at work."

"It's just a little something to celebrate your five hundreth lesson."

"I thought for a minute I'd lost you there but I guess the old stetho's on the blink."

"I told you not to drink all that coffee."

"I know I'm taking a long time but I'm trying to fry you an egg and the shell keeps breaking."

"Why did your nurse want to know my 'next-of-kin'?"

"Surely you can go bowling with Harvey another night?"

"Want me to get you a wig for your birthday?"

"Look at the fabulous tie I got you while I was buying this silly old coat."

"I gotta write a poem about Dad. What rhymes with 'el dummo'?"

"Okay, now shift your weight onto the left leg during the follow-through."

"If you don't keep quiet I'm gonna phone all your friends and tell them how old you really are."

"You wouldn't let me have a dog. You wouldn't let me have a cat!"

"The front row is yours!"

"You the guy who ordered the 'Breakfast Special'?"

"I'm telling you for the last time, I don't wanna go to a disco. I'm going to bed."

"All right, all right. So I'm five minutes late with the supper. You don't have to eat the plate."

"Is that your final answer?"

"Can you put my arm in a sling for a couple of weeks so I can get out of doing the dishes?"

"How do you expect to wash like that?"

"The paper's okay and the ink's okay. You left the 'w' out of 'twenty'!"

"Ma'am, the Captain has requested that you give
him a few minutes advance warning should
you wish to leave your seat during the flight."

"Whaddyer mean I should have told you?
I told you weeks ago."

"Gee Ralph, the party was yesterday!"

"Doc. it's a marvelous idea! You fill 'em up with flu
vaccine and put them on all the chairs in your waiting
room."

"I know you take a shower almost every day. You almost took one Monday, you almost took one Tuesday......"

"There you go! I forged your signature. You're in the Marines."

"How am I supposed to sleep with all that scrunching? If you must eat those things, take your teeth out."

'Wake up! Marcus Welby here is trying to saw off your leg.'

"Two brand new television shows starting this week. 'Lassie, The Six Million Dollar Dog' and 'I Love Bionic Lucy'."

"I guess things have changed since I was at school, Headmaster!"

"You gotta stop throwing food at Daddy."

"These fireplace logs are just pieces of a tree. Haven't you got any of the real plastic ones?"

"What are you taking? We're only going to the zoc."

"Where do I put my mouth?"

"If I can't afford to buy a really expensive birthday gift I don't buy anything at all. So I didn't get you anything."

"Been here long, Pop?"

"What?"

"Now you're in Grade 4, Daddy's not going to be able to help you with your homework anymore."

"Not another war movie!"

"The Doctor says he'll see the gentleman with the smallpox first."

"There's four clean socks in here. One blue, one brown, one green and one red."

"Yeah, well I guess if the Doc says to stay in bed for the rest of the day, I'd better stay."

"How can I throw in the towel before the bell for round one?"

"Next time your car won't start, try calling a mechanic."

"For the money I'm paying for this portrait, I hope you're getting beneath the surface and painting the real me."

"I didn't call you a 'shrimp'. I said, 'Can I get you anything to DRINK?'."

"I coulda sold a million albums by now if you hadn't made me take singing lessons."

"I can only say I'll let you know. I have another four hundred applicants to see."

"How come I never hear you say 'please' and 'thank-you'."

"This is my new boyfriend. Can he have something to eat?"

"Whaddyer mean, 'I'll be late for work'? It's six o'clock in the evening."

"He'll be okay! He overdosed on sunflower seeds."

"Good grief man! How does anyone swallow an electric toothbrush?"

"I think it needs some protein to give it more 'body'."

"Yeah, well your not exactly an oil painting yourself first thing in the morning."

"Are you sure he told you to stick a barometer in my mouth?"

"If you don't believe men came from monkeys, go and take a good look at your father."

"Did you make a blind date with someone named Yvonne?"

"There's not much here. The only description he can give us is red socks, brown shoes with black and white laces—one broken with the tips missing."

"Herman, here's your ax back. Now can I borrow your chain saw?"

"Of course it's dangerous. I didn't get to be a general without taking chances."

"Come on, don't waste my time. Get out of there."

"Mind your own business! This is how I like it."

"You told me to use my initiative if I needed money, so I sold your car."

"Try again, sir; that was my foot."

"Guess what Mike does for a living!"

"I guess we should have tried it on the rats first."

"You're the one guy we can trust in this cell for a couple of days 'til we get those bars fixed."

"Don't play with Grandpa's greasy hair just before suppertime."

"The bottom's dropped out of the market. I've lost 18 bucks."

"It's been postponed. He's got a headache."

"I can get a court order to stop you from teaching her to cook."

"Mom, why don't you get a divorce and marry someone with more money?"

"We implant this behind your left ear and you won't even know it's there."

"What made you give up the 'fight game'?"

"I can't go out tonight, Frank; I'm washing my hair."

"How was Africa?"

"I know you've been late for work twice this week. I still think it's stupid to sleep in the car!"

"I know you want to play Hamlet, but for this one television commercial you're a stick of celery."

"No, you can't wear it to school. Put it back on the wall."

"I am grateful! But I distinctly remember asking for a cheese sandwich."

"Herman fixed the washer!"

"I've unclogged the upstairs bath."

"So you dyed your hair and it turned green. You can't spend the rest of your life in this bathroom."

"Keep out! Keep out! K-E-E-P O-U-T."

"Of course your operation is 'absolutely necessary.' Without it I don't get a summer vacation."

"Dennis is a sweet sensitive guy, and if you don't let us get married he's gonna break both your legs."

223